Contents

Before footballs were invented . . . 4

The early days of football 7

The first real footballs 11

Modern footballs 18

Ten fascinating football facts . . . 20

Timeline 22

Index 24

To play football you need the right ball.

too small

too big

just right

These days most people have a football to play with.

In the old days, there were no real footballs.

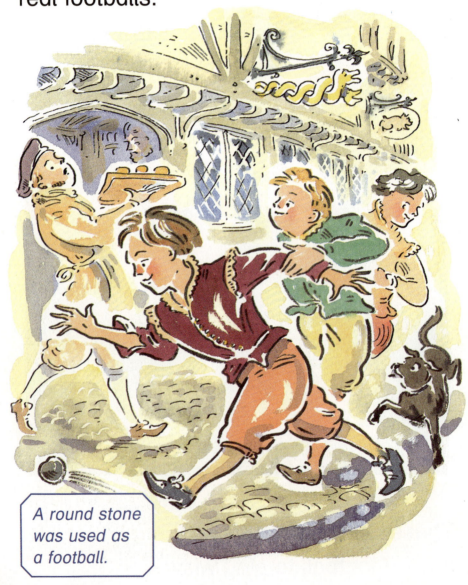

A round stone was used as a football.

Stones do not make very good footballs.

Then someone had an idea.

a butcher's shop

A pig's bladder could be used as a football.

A pig's bladder comes from inside a pig.

It does not hurt your foot when you kick a pig's bladder.

But a pig's bladder is not very strong.

Pigs' bladders do not make very good footballs.

Then someone had a better idea.

Pieces of leather were sewn around the pig's bladder.

This was the first real football.

pig's bladder

leather

 →

This ball was much better because it lasted longer.

But the pig's bladder inside still burst.

Then someone had the idea of using a rubber balloon instead of a bladder.

But this ball became very heavy when it soaked up the rain.

Kicking this ball could hurt your foot.

Then someone thought of using plastic instead of rubber.

Most modern footballs are made in Pakistan.

plastic sac

thin but strong leather

valve

plastic sac

The valve lets air into the ball.

 →  → →

The modern football is easier to play with and stronger.

It can be kicked further and faster.

Ten fascinating football facts

A ball has only ever burst once in an FA Cup Final – that was in 1946.

Years ago, goals in football did not have crossbars. (That must have made it much easier to score!)

In 1872, England played Scotland in the first official Soccer International.

When England won the World Cup in 1966, they played with a brown football.

Liverpool have played more games in Europe than any other club.

The oldest player in a football league match played in goal for New Brighton against Hartlepool, aged 52 years and 4 months!

In 1921 the rule was introduced that goalkeepers in international matches had to wear yellow jerseys.

100 years ago, a season ticket to watch West Bromwich Albion cost three shillings (15p).

The Chinese played football games at least 3000 years ago.

The first women's teams were formed in England in the 1880s.

Timeline

1600 | 1700

17th Century

The first footballs are inflated pigs' bladders, which often burst.

18th Century

Pieces of leather are sewn around the pigs' bladders, but the bladders still burst.

| 1800 | 1900 | 2000 |

19th Century

Footballs are still made of leather but the pigs' bladders have been replaced by rubber balloons. Footballs become very heavy because they soak up the rain.

20th Century

Footballs are made of very thin leather around an inflated plastic inner sac. They are stronger and more waterproof so that they don't soak up the rain.

Index

leather **10–11, 14, 17**

pig's bladder **7–14**

plastic sac **17**

rubber balloon **14–15**

stone **4–5**

valve **17**